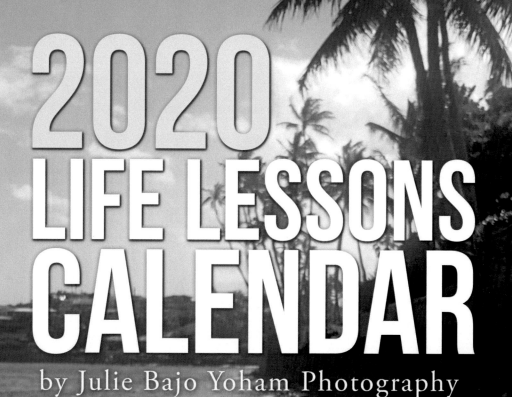

2020 LIFE LESSONS CALENDAR

by Julie Bajo Yoham Photography

JULIE BAJO YOHAM

To order additional copies of this book, contact:
Xlibris
1-888-795-4274
www.Xlibris.com
Orders@Xlibris.com

ISBN: Softcover   978-1-7960-6387-5
         EBook   978-1-7960-6388-2

Print information available on the last page

Rev. date: 10/30/2019

2020
LIFE LESSONS
CALENDAR

DEDICATION

Dedicated to my husband Daniel J Yoham and all my friends in Hawaii also who helped me along the way. To the future people who enjoy this book and are enlightened to live a beautiful life daily.

ACKNOWLEDGEMENT

Thank you to my mom Julia, Javier Vidal also and my husband Daniel J. Yoham for getting me through my LIFE entirely alive because of them

Thanks to Stg. Allen M, Lt. Eric H., Scott, Carey, and all my coworkers on the TV series and stage shows during the 90s when I was around acting teachers and casting agents. Thanks to you all from my heart. Much love to you all.

Besides the original Eddie, Leonard, Earle, Martha and Mama Rose and America, my mom for one Christmas and taxis in Waikiki I was Gigi goddess of love and light. Thanks so much for the ability to get to work. Casting and teachers Wayne, Margaret and Kireal the healer of the Universe for me for years on Oahu, Hawaii.

Also, Thanks to Joe Sr., Jr., Joe C., Dj David and Dwayne the best Dj's in my life, besides the original Richard Freeman who was a technical director in San Francisco during the 90s when I was around the theatre which was one of the greatest and best times of my life. My mentors and friends through the 90s and 2006. Thanks for the amazing times love you very much for your time and help for me. Thanks love always peace and loved always.

Thanks to Mike and Chris, my friends forever in my heart. Thanks to Artie Mitchell famous producer who took me to Maui first time I came back after his death in 1991. My life was never the same after Artie but I learned to heal myself and stayed there for a while. I am grateful to be alive and to have a beautiful experience in Hawaii. MAHALO AND ALOHA.

Thanks to the Maui writers conference in 1996 they were great teachers and inspirational for my writing my books while attending the week long teaching environment. Thanks so much for the kind attention to my writing all were amazing to me.

Thanks to Bo Dietl, my friend for several decades. Traveling to many locations together into the 90s and 2002. Wonderful friends made my life really fabulous, NY, Las Vegas, California and Florida. Thanks so much for the great times with incredible people along the way.

Thanks to Kenny and Sheila Fennel for friends forever who helped me in our wedding ceremony in 2017.

Thanks to Triva and Jamie Yoham for my wedding and friendship for years and all my families I am so grateful to you all.

Thanks to my dentist in Florida, California and Hawaii. I am clear and brain clean because of your work on my teeth. Thanks so much gratefully your patient forever. I write because they cleared out my head with surgery and anti-biotics for months to clear me. I am able to create my first book because I had surgery in 2019. FLORIDA CITY DENTAL. Thanks so much.

January 2020

SUNDAY	MONDAY	TUESDAY	WEDNESDAY	THURSDAY	FRIDAY	SATURDAY
29	30	31	1	2	3	4
5	6	7	8	9	10	11
12	13	14	15	16	17	18
19	20	21	22	23	24	25
26	27	28	29	30	31	1
2	3	NOTES				

January

❋

Healing >True Intention Is The Key >

The healers bank account is an intangible account of all the things we have done for others without expecting anything in return. Trusting in the Universal energy which sees all. We cannot control what others do to us but we have total control of our minds, bodies and enlightenment. Our choices prevail in the Universe it knows all some try to lie to us or the Universe without success. When we pass to the other side of dimensions we live our karmic choices we have made while alive. Choose wisely because our Earth school is where we return to continue learning the lessons for our enlightenment. We clear our chakras 1 through 7, and more until we are ready for the next dimension of energy. Our magic bank accounts filled with love energy carries us through our lives and beyond that. Be mindful of the choices you are making every step of the way it's your choice, only yours to make. We might return many times until we are truly enlightened as long as it takes for true deep insight into our minds bodies and spiritual being. We are surrounded by our other bodies, astral, mental and spiritual. It's all about the energy felt by everyone around us and the Universe.

February 2020

SUNDAY	MONDAY	TUESDAY	WEDNESDAY	THURSDAY	FRIDAY	SATURDAY
26	27	28	29	30	31	1
2	3	4	5	6	7	8
9	10	11	12	13	14	15
16	17	18	19	20	21	22
23	24	25	26	27	28	29
1	2	NOTES				

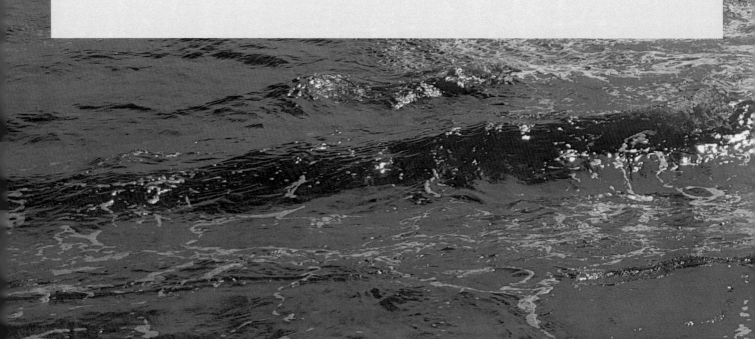

February

Forgiving.

Forgiveness is such a powerful force that most humans may never fully experience this very magic force of energy. It takes great courage to really forgive those who have done things against us. On a daily basis there are those who feel so sad inside they must upset those around them. The strongest, greatest people are capable of not only making everyone feel good about themselves but even those who go against all good judgment. Judgement not as in judging others but knowing exactly what to do to make good energy rise from their hearts to the cosmos affecting everything on the way up. This becomes more important of a reaction than any small ego boost or confronting type of energy. Only when you can truly experience this feeling can you actually call yourself a spiritual person.

March 2020

SUNDAY	MONDAY	TUESDAY	WEDNESDAY	THURSDAY	FRIDAY	SATURDAY
1	2	3	4	5	6	7
8	9	10	11	12	13	14
15	16	17	18	19	20	21
22	23	24	25	26	27	28
29	30	31	1	2	3	4
5	6	NOTES				

March

Spirituality > Spirituality is not a religion it lives inside all of us.

When we are born our spirit is part of us all and we are all part of the divine plan of the Universal intelligence that surrounds us with energy. We are all connected through studying and practice in faith we become powerful from the inside through knowledge. This is one of the most significant lessons I have learned it becomes less important to find external power. My strength comes from the source of all that is in the Universe. Our minds, bodies and spirits create our reality making our dreams come true. We all have spirit guides and angels who protect us from other dimensions. The external power is fun as in clothing, furnishings, automobiles all of those things bring pleasure. Equally we must exercise our internal power as well read diverse thinkers who have faith in ourselves and all that is power of the Universe. The creator gods, avatars, guardian angels I know they are part of all of us. Believe, I really know it to be true.

April 2020

SUNDAY	MONDAY	TUESDAY	WEDNESDAY	THURSDAY	FRIDAY	SATURDAY
29	30	31	1	2	3	4
5	6	7	8	9	10	11
12	13	14	15	16	17	18
19	20	21	22	23	24	25
26	27	28	29	30	1	2
3	4	NOTES				

April

Wisdom > Wisdom has nothing to do with age.

Each decade brings along lessons to learn from yet our free will gives every human a choice to repeat the same things if we don't learn to move up from the not knowing phase of life. Reality dictates that once the mind, body and spirit come into alignment the priorities drastically change. Each human individually must show itself to be worthy of knowing all. When they are enlightened instead of living inside of the ego which is a less powerful force of energy they ascend to a higher dimension of energy. Pretending to be in connection with this alignment is natural but much better to really be in it by choice. Living in the light and being kind to all living things becomes your nirvana when you get to this point it is Nirvana.

May 2020

SUNDAY	MONDAY	TUESDAY	WEDNESDAY	THURSDAY	FRIDAY	SATURDAY
26	27	28	29	30	1	2
3	4	5	6	7	8	9
10	11	12	13	14	15	16
17	18	19	20	21	22	23
24	25	26	27	28	29	30
31	1	NOTES				

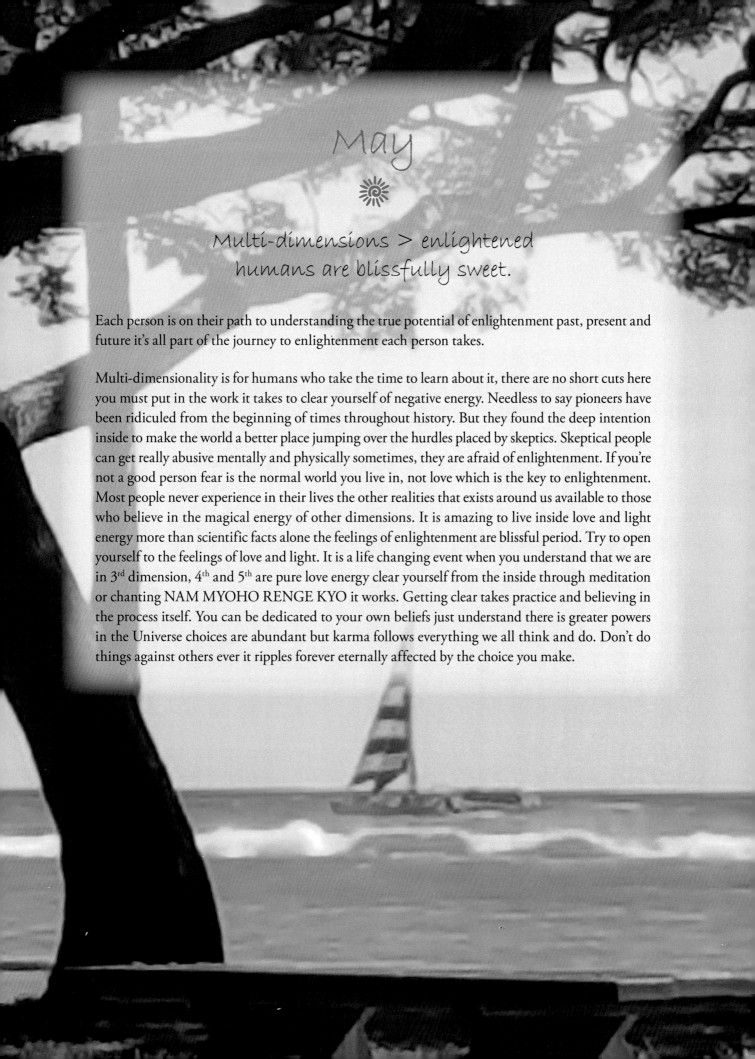

May

*

Multi-dimensions > enlightened humans are blissfully sweet.

Each person is on their path to understanding the true potential of enlightenment past, present and future it's all part of the journey to enlightenment each person takes.

Multi-dimensionality is for humans who take the time to learn about it, there are no short cuts here you must put in the work it takes to clear yourself of negative energy. Needless to say pioneers have been ridiculed from the beginning of times throughout history. But they found the deep intention inside to make the world a better place jumping over the hurdles placed by skeptics. Skeptical people can get really abusive mentally and physically sometimes, they are afraid of enlightenment. If you're not a good person fear is the normal world you live in, not love which is the key to enlightenment. Most people never experience in their lives the other realities that exists around us available to those who believe in the magical energy of other dimensions. It is amazing to live inside love and light energy more than scientific facts alone the feelings of enlightenment are blissful period. Try to open yourself to the feelings of love and light. It is a life changing event when you understand that we are in 3rd dimension, 4th and 5th are pure love energy clear yourself from the inside through meditation or chanting NAM MYOHO RENGE KYO it works. Getting clear takes practice and believing in the process itself. You can be dedicated to your own beliefs just understand there is greater powers in the Universe choices are abundant but karma follows everything we all think and do. Don't do things against others ever it ripples forever eternally affected by the choice you make.

June 2020

SUNDAY	MONDAY	TUESDAY	WEDNESDAY	THURSDAY	FRIDAY	SATURDAY
31	1	2	3	4	5	6
7	8	9	10	11	12	13
14	15	16	17	18	19	20
21	22	23	24	25	26	27
28	29	30	1	2	3	4
5	6	NOTES				

June

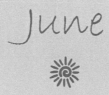

Strength > Strength means that we must be strong always.

We know that in this century the psychological discovery that in order to control a human they must first destroy the spirit it is the person I was in this reality until I got away from my family I finally flew high into my own beautiful reality and became enlightened throughout many years of studying, practice and beliefs in the process itself and intention is the key the pure heart works. My destroyers of pure love energy collapsed my every beautiful assets to control me until I woke up and left their abusive ways of life. When I returned many years later I was saddened to see they had not changed at all. Brutal evil lying disastrous people I had to cut them out of my life completely. It is the answer cut out the evil energies because it gets in the way of your enlightenment. They will eventually find their way too out of the bad energy life they currently live now. The mastermind energy is one of creating discourse or bad energy to control you, so be smart enough to get away from those who are unaware of the Universe and intelligent life. It isn't worth the waste of time some people will never get it in this lifetime it may take many lifetimes to become clear enough to enjoy a life as a really beautiful spirit on earth respecting all living beings equally as well as all life forms. We are better human beings when we live love energy and treat people as if you see the god/goddess in them. Our spirits connect to the ALL THAT IS continuously, be conscious of the effects you have on the reality you live in.

July 2020

SUNDAY	MONDAY	TUESDAY	WEDNESDAY	THURSDAY	FRIDAY	SATURDAY
28	29	30	1	2	3	4
5	6	7	8	9	10	11
12	13	14	15	16	17	18
19	20	21	22	23	24	25
26	27	28	29	30	31	1
2	3	NOTES				

July

Independence > Independence from judging
people, actions or past mistakes of others who have
wrongly treated me badly throughout my life.

We must learn from our Earth School lessons that affect us in large and small ways alike it all happens for a reason. Sometimes stepping back you can see the powerful good fortune inside the turmoil of life at times. Not knowing about the Universal energy that surrounds us all is living without a powerful tool of cause and effect and how it works. The creator gods gave us tools we just became too lost in the ego based life to notice the powerful forces of the Universe. We have the gift to manifest anything we wish to dream of and work towards step by step we can achieve anything we wish to have in this lifetime. Living in the light energy every second, minute, and day you can become clearer every day. When you are ready as a student suddenly the teachers appear to help you get there. Believe me it happened to me I was brought up by lost souls but I became the goddess of live and light energy in Hawaii over decades of studying and traveling there. The only thing I had to do was to protect myself from all bad energies to be able to give beautiful energy to those I performed for. The energy makes the difference of a fabulous memorable movement of my body through dancing for my audience over many decades. When the student is ready the teacher appears.

August 2020

SUNDAY	MONDAY	TUESDAY	WEDNESDAY	THURSDAY	FRIDAY	SATURDAY
26	27	28	29	30	31	1
2	3	4	5	6	7	8
9	10	11	12	13	14	15
16	17	18	19	20	21	22
23	24	25	26	27	28	29
30	31	NOTES				

August

✺

Life > The month I was personally born in.

Fortunately some of the greatest wisdom influences have stayed with me and made my life better. It has made me ponder life and as a result become a better person in every way.

What I would like to share this month is a simple and powerful meditation that has made a difference in my life, my world and how I am able to deal with adversity daily.

As much as possible take time out to be with your self in silence listening to your internal communications. No external sounds only concentrate on the positive thoughts that create your reality from the inside. While relaxed breathing consciously giving beautiful energy to the Universe asking the white light of healing energy to flow through your head to the Earth grounding you to the planet. Surrounding you with the white light energy visualize this, each chakra cleared crown, third eye, throat,

heart, solar plexus, stomach, and the root chakra connection to the Earth and Universe at the same time filling you with pure love energy and white light healing energy. It usually gives me chills from the inside out feeling connected to the ALL THAT IS.

Chakras are your body's energy points or center's wheels throughout the body balancing the etheric, physical and emotional, mental bodies that surround us. People actually feel the energy some even see the colors that are around the chakras. Smiling from the inside your pure heart brings the best results, shining from the heart chakra with pure love energy is amazing.

September 2020

SUNDAY	MONDAY	TUESDAY	WEDNESDAY	THURSDAY	FRIDAY	SATURDAY
30	31	1	2	3	4	5
6	7	8	9	10	11	12
13	14	15	16	17	18	19
20	21	22	23	24	25	26
27	28	29	30	1	2	3
4	5	NOTES				

September

Meditation > It works.

Another simple meditation is one I like to use daily is to create a star around me visualize it mentally and physically putting both arms out in front of me hands touching saying " Protect me in the front, protect me in the back " Hands touching in the back . Then hands at my sides turned upward fingers pushing the force from me I say " Push evil energy back to where it comes from . " " Let the beauty of the goddess of love and light energy flow through me bring beautiful things into my energy and let me affect people with my healing power to make our Universe a better place. " Enlightened people can feel the energy flow through the bodies it feels really beautiful and it shows through the physical body and all the other bodies that surround us all. Reaching out to the guardian angels that are always around us all. Asking them to protect us in every day life situations. Repeat daily as needed to feel the energies around you and feeling protected from harmful energies out there in our reality.

October 2020

SUNDAY	MONDAY	TUESDAY	WEDNESDAY	THURSDAY	FRIDAY	SATURDAY
27	28	29	30	1	2	3
4	5	6	7	8	9	10
11	12	13	14	15	16	17
18	19	20	21	22	23	24
25	26	27	28	29	30	31
1	2	NOTES				

October

Learning > Everyone is a teacher and a student on Earth School.

Some people affect more than others depending on their clarity to the Universal energy. We are all on Earth for different periods of time being conscious of how we affect others really helps to be the best possible self inside and externally as well.

We all build our characters, mold our personality and expand our minds. Through letting go of emotional blocks we experience freedom. With conscious effort we experience being filled with love . With conscious thoughts we make good decisions. By living with no regrets we are always moving forward. Drinking in every moment for the preciousness of the fleeting existence which is life. These are lessons I have learned to live, how I want to live my life. Try it you'll like it . It really does work just believe.

November 2020

SUNDAY	MONDAY	TUESDAY	WEDNESDAY	THURSDAY	FRIDAY	SATURDAY
1	2	3	4	5	6	7
8	9	10	11	12	13	14
15	16	17	18	19	20	21
22	23	24	25	26	27	28
29	30	1	2	3	4	5
6	7	NOTES				

November

Gratitude > Being grateful releases an energy the Universe recognizes as a pure energy.

The Universe is waiting to fulfill your every desire and the grateful energy is one that opens the door to your wishes coming true. I keep my mantras simple and to the point because life is complicated enough already daily. So here is a beautiful and easy meditation dedicated to the ALL THAT IS. Thank you for my life and loves I am feeling now and in the past.

Thank you for the air I breathe so necessary and crucial to live. The more pure the better but any air is life saving so thanks to the Universe for that.

Thank you for the opportunities presented to me daily I will give every day my best to fulfill my dreams coming true.

Thank you for the pleasures I have felt throughout my life and I hope to enjoy much more until I go to the next dimension of energy.

Thank you for the love I have felt from so many beautiful people I have known through all my decades of living in this lifetime and even the past lives I have had since it's all connected.

Thank you for the sun, the moon and the beautiful energy they give to me throughout my body, mind my spirit completely.

Thank you for my guides, spirit guides that surround me at all times always there for me. Thank you for the lessons even the painful ones there have been many through the years but I understand the lessons painful or blissful it was all part of the experience that has been my life I have grown from each moment and am still blessed to be alive after many close to death events. Thank you for the Light. Through it all the light gets me through it all. Light energy is love.

December 2020

SUNDAY	MONDAY	TUESDAY	WEDNESDAY	THURSDAY	FRIDAY	SATURDAY
29	30	1	2	3	4	5
6	7	8	9	10	11	12
13	14	15	16	17	18	19
20	21	22	23	24	25	26
27	28	29	30	31	1	2
3	4	NOTES				

December

Advancing > Find strength in the knowledge that you create your own reality.

If it doesn't feel right, change it . Whatever it takes, one step at a time just visualize it and do it as long as it doesn't hurt any living things in the process. One day you find yourself in your dream life doing the things that make you happy.

As we look forward to our magic energy human experience to cross over to another year full of growth we let go of old negative energy. Bad energy gets in the way of love and peaceful energy. Like oil and water one separates from the other it's our choice what we want to focus on. We are more powerful than we think we are, dream it and achieve it . Our thoughts are energy just like the actions we take, your thoughts literally create your reality and life evolves from that point of creation. Live your life beautifully be kind to people it is your karma you are creating every step of the way. Holding onto to anger or loss only hurts the person feeling it. I know people have hurt me but I choose to get that energy out of my life completely. It is the only way to survive getting away from all the negative energy brought on by others towards ourselves. This is one of the most significant lessons I have learned to live with. There is no room for the bad people in my life because life is short and I want to be happy as much as possible until I die. This difficult lesson is worth learning from and letting go of the negativity completely. It isn't easy but you will notice yourself accomplish more and live a more pure energy life this is the path to happiness I have found in my Journey to Enlightenment throughout this lifetime. That is my next book full of the stories I experienced in my life despite the evil energy out there I am happily living my life in 2020.Thanks so much. Peace and love to you all look inside yourself for the answer daily you are all you need to live.

The author Julie Bajo Yoham is a grateful photographer of the islands of Hawaii and to live there for many years. Mahalo and Aloha

Printed in the United States
By Bookmasters